THE SPOKEN WORD
A BBC Guide

Robert Burchfield
CHIEF EDITOR OF THE OXFORD ENGLISH DICTIONARIES

BRITISH BROADCASTING CORPORATION

Published by the
British Broadcasting Corporation
35 Marylebone High Street
London W1M 4AA

First published 1981
Reprinted 1981 (twice)
ISBN 0 563 17979 1

Printed in Great Britain by
BAS Printers Limited,
Over Wallop, Hampshire

CONTENTS

For E.A.K.

INTRODUCTION

English as she is murdered on radio became an issue once
more, after Alvar Lidell stamped his foot and blew the whistle in
The Listener.

Anne Karpf, *The Listener*, 3 January 1980

Background. This booklet results from a monitoring exercise of BBC
radio in mid-1979 undertaken by Professor Denis Donoghue, Mr
Andrew Timothy and myself at the invitation of Mr Aubrey Singer,
Managing Director of BBC Radio, and Mr Ian McIntyre, Controller
of Radio 3, the results of which were printed in a 24-page report
entitled *The Quality of Spoken English on BBC Radio* (BBC, October
1979). The exercise arose from a piece entitled 'Newsweeding' by the
well-known newsreader, the late Alvar Lidell, published in *The
Listener* on 5 April 1979, in which he claimed (not for the first time)
that the news was no longer read in an undistorted manner, but was
subject to 'widespread distortion, an endemic disease arising from
insinuation and implication'.

Conclusions. An exhaustive examination of the problem led me to
the following conclusions:

• There is abundant evidence that the standard of spoken English
broadcast on the BBC radio networks is in broad terms acceptable.
Many of those who fear that standards are dropping either lack a
historical perspective or place too much weight on occasional lapses or
on the mannerisms of individual broadcasters, and therefore fail to
recognize that most of the English spoken or read on the networks is
pleasantly presented in a variety of styles.

• Most of those who express concern about the state of the English
language at the present time seem to be unaware that more grievous or
more fundamental changes to the language have occurred at various

periods since it was first recorded in written form in the eighth century. Examples of such fundamental changes include the loss of grammatical gender in the late Old English and early Middle English period; the absorption of large numbers of foreign words at all periods since the days of Edward the Confessor and earlier; the great vowel shift at the beginning of the fifteenth century, when nearly every long vowel sound in the standard language radically changed its nature;[1] the severance of the home varieties of English into many overseas varieties, especially in North America and Australia; and during the twentieth century the adoption of English of varying degrees of adequacy as a lingua franca in virtually every country in the world.

Any argument based on the assumption that the changes occurring in the English language in Great Britain at present are more serious or more objectionable than those that have occurred in the last 1200 years is at least vulnerable and almost certainly false.

● It is important to distinguish certain features of spoken English from those of written English. For example, verbless sentences like 'This report from Paul Reynolds' and 'And so for the main points of the news again' are characteristic of broadcast English. Similarly the present tense often replaces the future tense in announcements about later programmes: 'At 8.30 Richard Stilgoe hunts through the BBC Sound Archives for the voices of those who have made history.' These are not 'faults' though they are often judged to be such by those whose standards are formed on the basis of written English.

● As there are probably more regional forms of speech in the United Kingdom than in any comparable geographical area in the world it is not suggested that every recommendation in *The Spoken Word* will commend itself to broadcasters everywhere in the country. Adjustments, especially in pronunciation, should be made as the need arises in each region.[2] It can no longer be assumed (as Alvar Lidell did) that

1 For example, *goose* which before 1400 was pronounced in the manner of modern English *close* (a close thing) gained its modern pronunciation when the great vowel shift occurred, as did *house* (before 1400 pronounced with the main vowel sound of modern English *moose*).

2 'Most people on Merseyside would wonder what the newsreader was about if he pronounced *mandatory* and *municipal* as recommended. Here it would always be the former with the stress on the second syllable and the latter with the stress on the

all broadcasters should speak R.P. (i.e. Received Pronunciation). Most BBC newsreaders and announcers in London do so, but there are exceptions, and many of the presenters, correspondents, weather forecasters, and so on, use entirely acceptable regional accents.

Main purpose. My main purpose has been to identify those elements of the spoken word that are to some degree (or more) debatable. In this booklet an attempt has been made to set down items of pronunciation, grammar, and vocabulary which lie in the controversial area and to provide a quick and decisive guide for announcers and presenters on the BBC networks and for others concerned with the preparation of the day-to-day scripts of BBC programmes.

If the matters set down below in tabulated form prove to have a wider relevance so much the better, but *The Spoken Word* has been prepared directly for broadcasters, in other words for those to whom the utterance of the English language is a matter of professional concern but for whom the circumstances of the day afford only brief rehearsal times or even, on occasion, no rehearsal at all.

Elocutionary aspects of the spoken word – whatever mixture of gravity, levity, or neutrality is appropriate to the reading of various kinds of broadcast English – are not dealt with here.

Acknowledgements. This booklet depends in large measure on the labours of others: the late Alvar Lidell, for whom the passage of time brought the desolation of linguistic change; Mr Ian McIntyre, Controller of Radio 3, for many courtesies and kindnesses; many announcers, presenters, and others within the BBC who allowed me to interview them or who commented on the typescript while it circulated within the BBC for about a year; Mr Graham Pointon, Pronunciation Adviser to the BBC; seven of my senior colleagues in the Oxford English Dictionary Department, Dr R. E. Allen, A. J. Augarde, Mrs L. S. Burnett, Miss J. M. Hawkins, A. M. Hughes, Miss S. Raphael, and Dr J. B. Sykes, all of whom assisted me during a monitoring examination of BBC radio programmes in July 1979; and the large number of listeners who made their views known to me on

---

third' – Manager, Radio Merseyside. 'If we pronounced everything the way suggested here our Northern listeners would feel we're a bunch of poofters (*restauran'*, *trai'*, etc.)' – Acting Programme Organizer, Radio Carlisle.

various phone-in programmes in this country, in America, and in New Zealand, or who sent me their views on what they took to be the singular and very culpable malpractices of the broadcasting media.

R.W.B.
Oxford
May 1981

A: PRONUNCIATION

'I can't understand what the young are saying any more.'
The Rt Hon. Edward Heath to the present
writer, BBC Nationwide studio, 6 June 1979

1 In what follows it is assumed that the speaker uses Received Standard English in its 1980s form. The form of speech recommended is that of a person born and brought up in one of the Home Counties, educated at one of the established southern universities, and not yet so set in his ways that all linguistic change is regarded as unacceptable. It is not intended to be a guide to the precise phonetic quality of individual sounds in the manner attempted in such standard works as A. C. Gimson's *Everyman's English Pronouncing Dictionary* (ed. 14, 1977). On the contrary, it is assumed that trained announcers and presenters will have little need of guidance in such matters but will be grateful to have access to a reference list of clear preferences.

2 It should be borne in mind that the pronunciation of a given word or class of words seldom changes in a period of less than fifty years, and that acceptance of such changes by all sections of the community may take even longer. For example:

armada: *c*. 1880 as in 'raider'; from *c*. 1930 as in 'harder'.

balcony: stressed on 2nd syllable *c*. 1825; on 1st syllable by *c*. 1890.

gynaecology: *c*. 1898 initial soft *g* only; till about 1930 optionally hard or soft *g*; from *c*. 1930 hard *g* only.

profile: *c*. 1908 2nd syllable as in 'feel'; now only as in 'file'.

rabies: *c*. 1903 three syllables like 'baby ease'; two-syllabled form first entered in the *Concise Oxford Dictionary* in 1964.

9

syndrome: *c.* 1919 three syllables like 'syncope'; now only two syllables.

3 All pronunciation problems may be referred to the BBC Pronunciation Unit. In particular, consult its daily bulletins for difficulties about the pronunciation of foreign or unfamiliar proper names like *Kabul, Khomeini, Managua, Nicaragua,* and *Tehran.* For the standard pronunciation of established proper names like *Blaenau Festiniog, Cirencester, William Cowper* (the poet), and *Erith,* consult G. M. Miller, *BBC Pronouncing Dictionary of British Names* (OUP, 1971). The standard authority for general vocabulary is *Everyman's English Pronouncing Dictionary,* edited by A. C. Gimson (J. M. Dent & Sons Ltd, ed. 14, 1977).

4 In the formal presentation of the news or of other scripted speech:
   (i)   Avoid the intrusive *r*:
                drawing   *not* draw-ring
                idea of   *not* idea-r-of
                law-abiding   *not* law-r-abiding
                But be careful to make correct liaisons, as in 'a pair‿of'.
   (ii)   Avoid the American[1] *-ar-*:
                *nec*essarily   *not* neces*sar*ily
                *tem*porarily   *not* tempo*rar*ily
   (iii) For words ending in *-eity,* as *deity, homogeneity, spontaneity,* use the sound in 'see' (dee-ity, etc.), *not* the sound in 'say'.
   (iv) Preserve *-ng-* (ŋ) in words like *length* and *strength.*[2]
   (v) Pronounce the unaccented syllable immediately before final *-ly*:
                particularly   *not* particu-ly
                regularly   *not* regu-ly
   (vi) Avoid the use of the obsolescent *-ors/-orf* sound in words like *cross, loss,* and *off.*

---

1 Now widely used in Britain, particularly by young people, but best avoided for the present in formal contexts.
2 C. P. Snow, *Coat of Varnish* (1979): 'In fact, she didn't drop her final *g*s: the only relic of that odd usage was that she wouldn't pronounce the *g* in strength.'

(vii) Be careful not to garble words like *deteriorate, disastrous* (*not* -ast-er-ous*), *government, library, quarter* (*not* kort-), *re-membrance* (*not* -mem-ber-ance), *secretary*, and *vulnerable* (*not* vun-).

(viii) Avoid the use of reduced forms like 'gunna, kinda, sorta, wanna' for 'going to, kind of, sort of, want to', fairly commonly found in informal, but undesirable in formal, speech.

(ix) Avoid the pronunciation of a final *g* in words like *bring, thing*, etc. (acceptable in certain forms of regional English but not in Received Standard).

(x) Use a short o in words ending in *-lve* (*absolve, dissolve, evolve, resolve, revolve(r)*, etc.), but a long o in words ending in *-lt* (*bolt, colt, dolt*, etc.).

5 *Preferred pronunciation: a select list*

To judge from the letters of listeners, words marked ▲ are the ones that give most offence when pronounced otherwise than as indicated below.[1] In each case the pronunciation preferred is the traditional one except in cases where this has been driven out or survives only in the speech of older people.

acoustic	-coo- (*not* -cow-)
adults	stress on 1st syllable
adversary	stress on 1st syllable
allies	stress on 1st syllable
Antarctic	first c fully pronounced
anti-	short final syllable (*not* as in *tie*)
apartheid	3rd syllable as in *hate*
apparatus	3rd syllable as in *rate*
applicable	stress on 1st syllable
Arctic	first c fully pronounced
aristocrat	stress on 1st (*not* 2nd) syllable
ate	rhymes with *bet*, not with *bait*

---

1 The pronunciations that are not recommended may well prevail, as time goes on, within a period of about half a century. Inclusion in this list normally means that the preferred pronunciations are in process of change at the present time or that they have now prevailed over those more usual at an earlier period in the present century.

capitalist	stress on 1st syllable
centenary	(sent*ee*nary)
centrifugal	stress on 2nd syllable[1]
centripetal	stress on 2nd syllable
cervical	stress on 2nd syllable with long i as in *like*
▲comparable	stress on 1st syllable[2]
▲composite	3rd syllable like *opposite* (*not* like *sight*)[3]
congratulatory	stress on 2nd syllable
conjugal	stress on 1st syllable
consummate	(verb) stress on 1st syllable; (adj.) stress on 2nd syllable
▲contribute	stress on 2nd syllable
▲controversy	stress on 1st syllable[4]
contumely	three syllables (*not* four);[5] stress on 1st syllable
data	1st syllable as in *rate*
decade	stress on 1st syllable
deficit	stress on 1st syllable
▲deity	1st syllable as in *see* (*dee*-ity)
derisive	2nd syllable as in *rice*
despicable	stress on 1st syllable[6]
deteriorate	-or- to be pronounced, not omitted
dilemma	1st syllable with short i, *not* as in *tie*

1 Nearly all young people now pronounce this and the following word with the stress on the third syllable, seemingly unaware of the existence of the traditional pronunciation.

2 The pronunciation with stress on the 2nd syllable arises by analogy with the verb *compare*.

3 The pronunciation that is not recommended is commonly used by speakers from the north of England.

4 Thus following the pattern of *matrimony* rather than of *monotony*. Competing patterns exist for many such four-syllabled words; of such words *controversy* and *kilometre* are at present nicely balanced. One of the two forms of pronunciation will become established as the usual form in due course. Meanwhile the traditional stressing should be observed.

5 Earlier in the century frequently pronounced as four syllables (con-tum-e-ly).

6 In informal speech ('How despicable!', 'That fellow's behaviour is despicable!') the stress is very commonly placed on the second syllable. ('Makes it sound much more vicious!' – Andrew Timothy.)

diphtheria	*ph* pronounced (f) not (p)
disastrous	see § 4 (vii) above
disputable	stress on 2nd syllable
▲dispute	stress on 2nd syllable[1]
dissect	1st syllable dis-, *not* as in *dice*
▲distribute	stress on 2nd syllable
dour	to rhyme with *poor* not *power*
economic	1st syllable equally acceptable pronounced as in *deck* or as in *equal*[2]
envelope	1st syllable as in *ten*, *not* as *on*
etcetera	etset-, *not* eks-
exquisite	stress on 1st syllable
February	(*feb*-roor-i) *not* (*feb*-you-)
fetid	1st syllable as in *set*, not *feet* (except when spelt in the older style *foetid*)
fifth	2nd f fully pronounced
furore	pronounce as three syllables
genuine	never (except humorously) to rhyme with *swine*
▲government	1st n fully pronounced (*and never* guv-ment)
guerrilla	can, but not easily, be distinguished from *gorilla* by using in the 1st syllable an unstressed form of the vowel in *guest*
half-past	first element fully pronounced (*not* har-past)
harass	stress on 1st syllable
harassment	stress on 1st syllable
hectare	2nd syllable as in *air*
hegemony	g as in *gun*, stress on 2nd syllable[3]
homogeneous	1st syllable as in *Tom*[4]

1 For both noun and verb. The noun is often heard with stress on the first syllable in imitation of northern dialects where it is much more widespread than in the south and midlands. The influence of usage by northern trade union leaders is tending to bring the form with initial stress into prominence.

2 But it is important to be consistent once the choice is made.

3 Throughout the present century the pronunciation has been unstable; often stressed on first syllable, sometimes with long e as in *see*, and also often with g pronounced as in *gin*.

4 Not to be confused with *homógenous*, a different word.

13

homosexual	1st syllable as in *Tom*[1]
hospitable	stress on 1st syllable
hotel	*h* to be pronounced (a, *not* an, before)
inherent	2nd syllable as in *here*
integral	stress on 1st syllable
internecine	stress on 3rd syllable, pronounced as *knee*; 4th syllable as in *sign*
intricacy	stress on 1st syllable
inveigle	2nd syllable as in *way*
irreparable	stress on 2nd syllable
irrevocable	stress on 2nd syllable
January	(*jan*-yoor-i)
▲jewellery	jewel-ry *not* (joo-ler-y)
▲kilometre	stress on 1st syllable[2]
lamentable	stress on 1st syllable
launch	pronounce as *law* (not as *branch*)
length	ng to be pronounced as in *sing* (*not* 'lenth')
longevity	(lon-jevity) *not* (-gev-)
longitude	ng as in *lunge*
lour (verb)	to rhyme with *hour* not *lower*
mandatory	stress on 1st syllable
medicine	two syllables (med-sin)*not* three (med-i-sin)[3]
metallurgy	stress on 2nd syllable[4]
migraine	1st syllable as in *see*
municipal	stress on 2nd syllable
nuclear	not to be pronounced like *circular*
occurrence	2nd syllable as *current*, *not* as *discursive*

---

1 The abbreviated form *homo*, which would not normally occur in scripted speech, is usually pronounced (home-o).
2 The form with stress on the second syllable (kilómetre) is increasingly heard. It is presumably modelled on words like *barometer* and *speedometer*. Other words beginning with *kilo-* (*kilogram, kilolitre*, etc) are always pronounced with the stress on the first syllable.
3 But the word is so often pronounced as three syllables, even by doctors, that the use of the three-syllabled form may go unnoticed if used consistently.
4 Still pronounced with stress on the first syllable by older people.

ophthalmic	*ph* pronounced (f) *not* (p)
opus	long o as in *hope*
pariah	stress on 2nd syllable, pronounced as *Isaiah*[1]
pejorative	stress on 2nd syllable
peremptory	stress on 2nd syllable
plastic	1st syllable short as in *bombastic*, not as in *plaster*
pomegranate	four syllables (pom-i-gran-at) *not* three
precedence	stress on 1st syllable (same sound as *press*)
preferable	stress on 1st syllable as in *preface*
▲primarily	stress on 1st syllable; other syllables unstressed
privacy	short i as in *river*
pronunciation	avoid the modern tendency to say pron*ou*nciation
quandary	stress on 1st syllable[2]
recognize	g fully pronounced
recondite	stress on 1st syllable[3]
remembrance	see § 4 (vii) above
reputable	stress on 1st syllable
▲research	stress on 2nd syllable (noun and verb)
restaurant	final t silent
scenario	initial (s), 2nd syllable stressed and with sound of *car*[4]
secretary	(sec-re-tree) *not* (sec-e-tree or sec-e-tair-ee)
sheikh	pronounced the same as *shake*
sonorous	stress on 2nd syllable[5]
Soviet	long o as in *stove*[6]
▲spontaneity	3rd syllable as in *see* (spon-tan-*ee*-ity)

---

1 Still pronounced by older people, especially Anglo-Indians, like *carrier*.
2 Even as late as the 1920s stressed on the second syllable which was pronounced like *dairy*.
3 Many educated speakers stress this word on the second syllable: only a Gallup poll would reveal which of the two pronunciations is the more usual, but no one can question the acceptability of the pronunciation recommended here.
4 Until the late 1920s the first syllable was pronounced (shay-).
5 This traditional pronunciation is now fairly quickly being replaced by one with the first syllable stressed (and this o short).
6 But the common pronunciation with short o as in *sovereign* is equally acceptable in educated use.

status	1st syllable as in *rate*
strength	ng to be pronounced as in *sing* (*not* 'strenth')
subsidence	stress on 2nd syllable, pronounced like *side*[1]
suffragan	hard g as in *gun*
surveillance	pronounce the *l* as in *veil*; it is not silent
▲ temporarily	stress on 1st syllable; other syllables unstressed
trait	final t silent
unprecedented	2nd syllable like *press*
untoward	w fully pronounced, 3rd syllable as in *ward*
vagary	stress on 1st syllable, pronounced as *vague*
vitamin	1st syllable as in *wit*
zoology	(zo-*ol*-ogy), 1st syllable with long o as in *zone*[2]

1 The traditional pronunciation – just. The form with stress on the first syllable (influenced by *residence* and *subsidy*) is now common.

2 The practitioners of the subject, especially those more concerned with the animals themselves than with nomenclature and etymology, frequently use both this pronunciation and the form with initial zoo- with apparent indifference.

B: VOCABULARY

Standard work of reference: *The Oxford Paperback Dictionary*, edited by Joyce M. Hawkins (1979), from which much of the material in section (iii) is drawn.

(i) *Clichés*

> 'Who you are and what you would are out of my welkin; I might say "element", but the word is overworn.'
>
> Shakespeare, *Twelfth Night*

The following clichés, among others, should be avoided:
at the end of the day
at this moment in time
at this point in time
in this day and age
no way
ongoing
scenario
situation (preceded by a noun or phrase: see section (iii) below)
you name it.[1]

(ii) *Inflation or modishness of diction*[2]

---

1 This and the next list could be extended indefinitely. Eric Partridge's *Usage and Abusage* (1942) s.v. *cliché* provides a list that occupies twenty-five pages, each of two columns.

2 A feature writer in *The Times* (29 December 1980) neatly drew attention to unnecessary inflation of diction in an article about a party of VIPs who were being shown round a new building in Dundee. 'The VIPs had two guides: the estates officer (who was an architect) and the doorman-cum-custodian. On reaching an emergency exit both guides spoke at once. The architect said: "That gives access to the exterior space"; the custodian said: "Yon door gies ootside."'

Use the word(s) in the right-hand column:

Avoid	*Prefer*
affluent	rich
assassinate[1]	kill, murder
commence	begin, start
crucial	important
currently	now, at present
donate	give
Draconian	severe, harsh, cruel
finalize	finish, complete
fresh (fighting in Beirut, talks, etc.)	re-express, using 'again', 'new' or 'renewed'
gay	homosexual
hero (in sport)	best player, athlete, etc.
hospitalize	admit to hospital
industrial action	specify the type (strike, work-to-rule, overtime ban, etc.)
literally	*rephrase*
massive	big, extensive
meet with	meet
normalize	restore to normal
participate	take part in
probe	go into, explore, examine; (as noun) investigation, etc.
proceed	go
request	ask
subsequently	later
terminate	end
tragedy (in sport)	*rephrase*
utilize	use

(iii) *Individual words*

■ Acceptable even in formal broadcasts
△ Avoid if possible

---

1 Unless the victim is a monarch, head of state, or the like.

agree:　　■　(transitive) to approve as correct or acceptable, e.g. *the tax inspector has agreed your allowances.*

aggravate:　■　1. To make worse or more serious, e.g. *Everything is being done by the bureaucrats to aggravate the discomfort* (E. Waugh).

　　　　　　△　2. To annoy, e.g. *Your behaviour aggravates him.*

ain't:　　　am not, is not, are not, has not, have not.

　　　　　　△　Avoid in standard speech except in humorous use, e.g. *she ain't what she used to be.*

alternative:　■　One of two or more[1] possibilities, e.g. (an uncontested use) *There are only two alternatives*; (disputed by a minority of people) *Of the several alternatives I prefer the one that causes the least congestion.*

anticipate:　■　1. To take action before someone else has had time to do so, e.g. *Others may have anticipated Columbus in the discovery of America.*

　　　　　　■　2. To notice what needs doing and take action in advance, e.g. *anticipate someone's needs*, provide for them in advance; *the boxer anticipated the blow*, saw it coming and blocked it.

　　　　　　△　3. To expect, e.g. *We anticipate that it will rain tomorrow.*

around:　　meaning 'about, approximately (at)', more usual in the US than in Britain. *Be here about 5 o'clock* (GB)/*Be here around 5 o'clock* (US); *there were about 50 people present* (GB)/*there were around 50 people present* (US).

compose:　　see *comprise*.

comprise:　■　1. To consist of, contain, e.g. *A full pack comprises 52 cards.*

　　　　　　△　2. To form, to make up, e.g. *The four submarines comprising the nuclear deterrent.*[2] Do not confuse

---

1 Vigorously resisted by listeners but impossible to avoid in many contexts.
2 This use is described by Fowler/Gowers (1965) as 'a wanton and indefensible weakening of our vocabulary'.

with *compose*, which in such contexts needs to be followed by *of*, e.g. *The group was composed of 20 students*; *The United Kingdom is composed of Great Britain and Northern Ireland*. It is incorrect to say *it was comprised of 20 students*.

data: often used with a singular verb (like 'information'), e.g. *the data is here*, but it is by origin a Latin plural (the singular is *datum*) and should be used (like 'facts') with a plural verb, *the data are here*.

decimate: ■ 1. To destroy one tenth of.

△ 2. To destroy a large proportion of.

deny: see *refute*.

deprecate: ■ To express disapproval of, e.g. *The plan to build a nuclear power station near London is to be deprecated*.

This word should be carefully distinguished from *depreciate* 'to diminish in value', e.g. *If the nuclear power station is built, house prices in the area are certain to depreciate*.

depreciate: see *deprecate*.

dilemma: ■ 1. A choice between two alternatives both of which are undesirable, e.g. *They were in the dilemma of either violating the Constitution or losing a golden opportunity*.

△ 2. A problem or difficult choice, e.g. *What to do with one's spare time is a modern dilemma*.

disassociate: use *dissociate*.

disinterested: ■ 1. Unbiased, not influenced by self-interest, e.g. *In the debate about Scottish nationalism the American was a disinterested observer*.

△ 2. Uninterested, uncaring, e.g. *The children were disinterested in their work*.[1]

due to: The phrase is often used like *because of*, e.g. *play was stopped, due to rain*. This usage is incorrect and

---

[1] Sense 2 attracts more unfavourable comment from listeners than any other word in this list with the possible exception of *hopefully*.

due to should be used only adjectivally with a noun (often after a linking verb), e.g. *the stoppage was due to rain.*

In a sentence like *She is entitled to all the respect due to a distinguished scholar* no problem arises: here *due* is an adjective followed by a preposition, not part of a complex preposition.

enormity: ■ 1. Great wickedness; a serious crime, e.g. *Titus whistled. He saw at once the enormity of what I had done.* In the plural: *I have got to the stage of disliking Randolph which is really more convenient than thinking I liked him and constantly trying to reconcile myself to his enormities* (E. Waugh).

△ 2. Enormous size, hugeness, e.g. *the enormity of their task.*

flaunt: ■ To display proudly or ostentatiously, e.g. *Everyone on the south terrace seemed to be flaunting a Scottish flag.*

△ Do not confuse with *flout* 'to disobey openly and scornfully', e.g. *The British administration accused the Zanla guerrilla army of deliberately flouting* (not 'flaunting') *the terms of the ceasefire.*

flout: see *flaunt.*

following: △ Do not use instead of *after* or *as a result of*; it is poor syntax and obscures the sense, as in *Police have arrested a man following extensive inquiries.*

hopefully: ■ 1. In a hopeful way, e.g. *he set to work hopefully.*

△ 2. It is hoped (that); let us hope, e.g. *Hopefully they will be available in the autumn.*[1]

imply: ■ To suggest without stating directly, to hint, e.g. *By saying that I should have known better he implied that I was an ignorant fool.* This word should be carefully distinguished from *infer*,[2] which means

---

[1] Used only by the brave or by young people unaware of public hostility to the use. Fanatically opposed by purists.

[2] A. P. Herbert in *What a Word!* (1935) brought out the distinction in an anecdote;

'to reach an opinion from facts or reason, to deduce', e.g. *I inferred from what he said that it was quite a long way to the nearest garage.*

infer: see *imply*.

interface: ■ 1. A surface forming a common boundary between two portions of matter or space, e.g. *The interface of the two liquids in the axial line.*

■ 2. An apparatus designed to connect two scientific devices, etc., e.g. *If you want to use one of the IBM languages on an ICL machine you will need to have an interface to make the two systems compatible.*

△ 3. Common ground or a boundary between two systems, disciplines, etc., e.g. *The interface of the Renaissance was the meeting of medieval pluralism and modern homogeneity* (McLuhan).

ironical: ■ 1. Expressing or suggesting irony, e.g. *Boyle . . . paid, in his preface, a bitterly ironical compliment to Bentley's courtesy* (Macaulay).

△ 2. Strange, noteworthy, paradoxical, e.g. *It is ironical that the Russians are using American components in some of their armaments.*

Similarly, the adverb *ironically* should not be used (as it often is) to mean 'as a matter of interest', 'strangely'.

latter: ■ The one mentioned second of two things. When referring to the last of three or more, *the last*, not *the latter*, should be used.

lay: Do not confuse *lay* (= put down; past tense *laid*) with *lie* (= recline; past tense *lay*).

■ Correct uses: *go and lie down*; *she went and lay down*; *please lay it on the floor*; *they laid it on the floor*.

△ Incorrect use is *go and lay down*.

'If you see a man staggering along the road you may *infer* that he is drunk, without saying a word; but if you say "Had one too many?" you do not *infer* but *imply* that he is drunk.'

lie: see *lay*.

loan (verb): △ e.g. *Will you loan me a book, please?* Correct use is *lend*.

militate: ■ To serve as a strong influence, e.g. *Several factors militated against the success of our plan.*
Distinguish this word carefully from *mitigate*. *Militate* is from Latin *militare* 'to serve as a soldier', and *mitigate* from Latin *mitigare* 'to moderate, lighten, alleviate'.

mitigate: ■ To make less intense or serious or severe, e.g. *Caesar interceded to mitigate the severity of the punishment.*
Distinguish this word carefully from *militate*.

ongoing: see *situation*.

p (abbreviation of 'penny', 'pence'): say 'pence' (not *pea*), or 'penny' if the amount is 1p.

parameter: The word has many abstruse technical senses in which it is correctly used, e.g. *Input parameters are included to specify page width and length; the density function for this variable will contain two parameters, μ and σ, which are the population mean and standard deviation respectively.*

△ This word should not be confused with *perimeter*, nor is it advisable in spoken English to use it in non-technical contexts as a simple synonym (in the plural) of *limits* or *boundaries*, though it frequently appears used thus in print, e.g. *The considerable element of indeterminacy which exists within the parameters of the parole system.*

portentous: ■ Foreboding some extraordinary and (usually) calamitous event; ominous, e.g. *an event more portentous than a mere dream.*
Distinguish this word from *pretentious*.

prestigious: 1. (*obsolete use*) Cheating, deluding, deceitful (from late Latin *præstigiosus* 'full of tricks, deceitful').
■ 2. Having or showing prestige, e.g. *he belongs to the*

23

most prestigious club in London.[1]

pretentious: Showy, pompous, e.g. *his pictures are clever, but a little more pretentious.*

Distinguish this word from *portentous.*

pristine: ■ 1. Ancient, primitive, old and unspoiled, e.g. *a sage of some pristine era.*

△ 2. Fresh as if new, e.g. *the ground was covered with a pristine layer of snow.*

protagonist: ■ 1. The principal character is a story or incident, e.g. *Some say that Iago is the protagonist in Verdi's Otello; Tony Benn is regarded as the protagonist of the Labour Left.*

△ 2. One who advocates or supports something (the opposite of *antagonist*), e.g. *Newton Aycliffe is a depressing place which even the protagonists of New Towns cannot be very fond of.* (This use arises from a false interpretation of the first three letters of the word as the prefix *pro-*, opposite to *anti-*, whereas the true etymon of the first element is Greek *prōt-os* 'first'.)

refute: ■ To prove that (a statement or opinion or person) is wrong, e.g. *By going over the evidence point by point he was able to refute his opponent's arguments.*

△ Sometimes incorrectly used to mean 'to deny, to repudiate', e.g. *I refute that. I wasn't even there.*

responsibility: A rebel group or band of terrorists is often described in newspapers and in news bulletins as 'claiming responsibility for (an outrage)'. There are more neutral ways of expressing the same idea, e.g. *The — say they were responsible; the — say* (or *admit*) *that they shot the policeman.*

seasonable: ■ Suitable for the time of year, in keeping with the season, e.g. *Hot weather is seasonable for August; he loved the seasonable mince pies that his aunt cooked at Christmas.*

---

1 Rearguard opposition to this use can now be ignored.

Distinguish from *seasonal* 'occurring at or associated with a particular season', e.g. *sheep-shearing is seasonal work; the seasonal migration of geese.*

seasonal: see *seasonable*.

situation: In use with a preceding noun or noun phrase since the 1920s, often in contexts where it is totally redundant, but now heard with increasing dismay and resentment by many listeners. Examples: *go through a crisis situation; not a loan but a standing credit situation; another no-win situation; an ongoing marketing situation; an ongoing political situation.* The phrase an *ongoing situation* should be avoided at all times.

thankfully: ■ 1. In a thankful way, e.g. *He accepted the food thankfully.*

△ 2. Let us be thankful (that), e.g. *Thankfully, the weather was fine.*[1]

transpire: ■ 1. (Of information, etc.) to leak out, to become known, e.g. *No details of the contract were allowed to transpire; after a few days it transpired that there had been collusion between the two parties.*

△ 2. To happen, e.g. *We'll see what transpires at the meeting.*

---

1 This use (a 'sentence adverb') is parallel to that of *hopefully* (see above), which attracts so many unfavourable comments from listeners. Other sentence adverbs, especially *important(ly)* in the phrase *more important(ly)*, are not objected to.

C. GRAMMAR

'I don't understand why children are not taught grammar.'

Caller on *Tuesday Call*,
Radio 4, 20 November 1979

'I am cantankerous ... about cooking and theology and clothes and grammar and dogs.'

Evelyn Waugh

Recommended books:

C. T. Onions, *An Advanced English Syntax* (ed. 6, 1932, or later editions).

E. Gowers' revision of H. W. Fowler's *A Dictionary of Modern English Usage* (OUP, ed. 2, 1965).

G. Leech and J. Svartvik, *A Communicative Grammar of English* (Longman, 1975).

English grammar is a complicated system never quite mastered even by the best speakers of English. The best writers and speakers avoid grammatical solecisms by keeping clear of areas which contain problems that would reveal their own uncertainties.

Many attempts have been made since Anglo-Saxon times to produce an agreed body of rules governing the operation of English sentences. The formalization of grammatical rules reached what was felt to be a state of near-perfection in the eighteenth century: grammarians analysed sentences into subject and predicate, clauses, moods, and so on. For various reasons the formal teaching of grammar in schools has now dwindled, sometimes it would seem almost to vanishing point. At the same time extraordinarily diverse modes of analysing English grammar have become fashionably established in the universities – transformational grammar, systemic grammar, and so on – especially in America but also in other English-speaking countries.

The sections that follow are largely restricted to negative aspects of grammar – which constructions are unacceptable or are best avoided – or to phrases or sentences in which one of two or more possibilities is preferable.

The evidence was compiled during the period when I monitored many BBC radio programmes (June/July 1979), supplemented by letters or questions received from members of the general public, and in particular in response to a 'Tuesday Call' programme entitled 'The Queen's English' in which I participated on 20 November 1979.

Naturally, the kind of usage that is acceptable in informal broadcasts, such as unscripted interviews, is different from that desirable in formal broadcasts, especially news bulletins. I have therefore adopted the following classifications, using a system of stars to indicate total or partial unacceptability in the ways indicated.

★★★   Unacceptable uses in any circumstances.

★★   Uses resisted by listeners but permissible in informal English.

★   Debatable features: preferences provided.

Some of the illustrative examples are taken from the works of modern writers like C. P. Snow, Iris Murdoch, and Graham Greene. Others are invented.

★★★   UNACCEPTABLE USES IN ANY CIRCUMSTANCES

1 *False concord*:

(i) in sentences:

There's two birds in the nest. (*Correctly*: *There are* two birds in the nest.)

Every one of those present *were* members of the union. (*Correctly*: *Every one* of those present *was a member* of the union.)

The nature of his injuries *are* not known. (*Correctly*: *The nature* of his injuries *is* not known.)

One of the stolen cars *were* not recovered. (*Correctly*: *One of* the stolen cars *was* not recovered.)

Someone has left *their* umbrella behind. (*Correctly*: *Someone* has

27

left *his*[1] umbrella behind.)

The jury hasn't been able to reach *their* verdict. (*Correctly*: *The jury hasn't* been able to reach *its* verdict. or[2] *The jury have not* been able to reach *their* verdict.)

(ii) classical plurals construed as singulars, e.g. *criteria, data, media, phenomena, strata.* Correct examples are as follows:

The media often display (*not* displays) a sensational approach to events.

This particular stratum (*not* strata) of society.

A phenomenon (*not* a phenomena) of considerable importance.

The criteria for distinguishing between good and bad poems are (*not* is) complex.

Numerical data are (*not* is) obtainable from the customs office.

2 *Failure to use the oblique case of pronouns*

Incorrect use: Between you and I (*correctly* between you and me).

He will give another chance to you and I (*correctly* me).

The message was intended for we broadcasters (*correctly* us broadcasters).

Correct use of the oblique case is shown in the following:

He loved and cherished my brother and me.

The gods have some treat in store for Lizzie and me (Iris Murdoch).

What will become of all us poor fellows on higher seas? (William Golding).

3 *Hanging or unattached participles*

The participle should normally have a proper 'subject of reference'. C. T. Onions said that 'a sentence like the following is incorrect because the word to which the participle refers grammatically is not that with which it is meant to be connected in sense':

---

1 It is possible, of course, that some people use *their* in such a sentence to avoid the awkwardness of *his or her*.

2 In formal English, collective nouns should normally be treated as grammatically singular, e.g. *the government is, the cabinet has, the union claims*, etc. In informal English both singular and plural constructions are acceptable (*The cabinet has decided where the new airport is to be built; the committee have dispersed for the summer*).

Born in 1850, *a part* of his education was received at Eton.
(*Correctly*: *Born* in 1850, *he* received part of his education at Eton.)
Similarly,

Calling upon him last summer, he kindly offered to give me his copy.
(*Correctly*: When I called . . .)

Being stolen, the Bank of England refused to honour the note.
(*Correctly*: The note being stolen, the Bank of England refused to honour it.)

When the unexpressed subject is indefinite it is permissible to use such constructions, e.g.

Roughly speaking they are identical.

Taking everything into consideration our lot is not a happy one.
In both cases an indefinite 'one' is implied: 'If one were to speak roughly', 'If one takes everything into consideration'.

The standard use of a participle is shown in: *Walking back I looked into my various pools* (Iris Murdoch).

4 Confusion of 'less' and 'fewer'

The word *less* is correctly used of things that are measured by amount (e.g. *to eat less butter, to use less fuel*). Its use of things measured by number is incorrect (e.g. *we need less workers*; correct usage is *fewer workers*).

The correct use of both *less* and *fewer* is illustrated in this sentence: *This beer has less body and less taste but fewer calories.*

5 Wrong participles

He was *sat* there (*correctly* sitting).

He was *stood* there (*correctly* standing).

He stood *leant* against the mantelpiece (*correctly* leaning).

We want this *changing* (*correctly* we want this changed).

This needs *changed* (*correctly* this needs changing).

6 Inability to carry through a sentence with 'one' as the subject

The pronoun *one* should be maintained throughout a sentence in which it forms the subject,[1] e.g.

One's best hope is to get into one of those 'holes' where one's two

---

1 In American English, however, 'one . . . his' is commonly found.

neighbours are eagerly engaged elsewhere, so that one can concentrate upon one's plate (Iris Murdoch).[1]

7 Confusion of 'more' and 'most'

The word *more* is correctly used when comparing only two people or things; conversely, *most* should not be used of comparison between two (e.g. *The two speakers were so angry that it was difficult to tell which of them was the more* (not *most*) *rational*).

★★ USES RESISTED BY LISTENERS BUT PERMISSIBLE IN INFORMAL ENGLISH

1 Preposition at end

Normally a preposition precedes the word it governs (he lives *in* a council house, he was hit *by* a bullet) but there are some circumstances in which it may or even must appear at the end of a clause or sentence.

(i) *Relative clauses*: You can't imagine the kind of horrors (that) he saved us *from* (Graham Greene).

A fear not exactly of James but of something that James stood *for* (Iris Murdoch).

(ii) *Wh*-questions:[2] Which hotel is he staying *at*?
Who are you voting *for*?

More formally: *At* which hotel is he staying?
For whom are you voting?

(iii) *Wh*-clauses: What I'm certain *of* is that the 1980s will be more dangerous than the 1970s.
What I am hoping *for* is a letter in tomorrow's post.
Let us see what it amounts *to*.

(iv) *Exclamations*: What a shocking state you are *in*!

(v) *Passives*: The doctor was sent *for*.

(vi) *Infinitive clauses*: There is nothing to be afraid *of*.
He is a nice person to work *for*.

These rules, which eluded Fowler's careful analysis, nevertheless

---

1 A rather extreme example selected to make the point clear.
2 *Wh* is used as a convenient abbreviation of *what*, *where*, *which*, *who*, and other pronouns and conjunctions beginning with *wh*.

support his general statement: 'It was once a cherished superstition that prepositions must be kept true to their name and placed before the word they govern in spite of the incurable English instinct for putting them late . . . If the final preposition that has naturally presented itself sounds comfortable, keep it.'

Naturally it is desirable to avoid complicated sentences like 'What did you bring that book I didn't want to be read to out of up for?' (attributed to a small girl who found that her mother had brought upstairs a book she did not like).

2 *Use of 'like' as a conjunction*
Grammarians[1] used to instruct readers never to use 'like' as a conjunction, except in a few humorous expressions (e.g. 'like the man said', 'If you knew Susie like I know Susie'), but modern writers regularly use this construction, especially when the verb is repeated in the same sentence:

> *Some girls change their lovers like they change their winter clothes* (Graham Greene).
>
> *They didn't talk like other people talked* (Martin Amis).

3 *Verbless sentences*
The occasional use of verbless sentences in broadcasts is acceptable (see p. 6). They are also commonly found in good fiction: *Another sunny day. Still no letters* (Iris Murdoch). *They could play with the harmony of repetitiveness. Which they had done* (C. P. Snow).

4 *Use of the present tense for the future tense*
The present tense in broadcast announcements, especially in trailers, often replaces the future tense (see p. 6). Such substitutions are acceptable both in the spoken language and in written analogues (as in the *Radio Times*).

5 *Emphasis on minor words, especially the indefinite and definite article*

---

1 And other writers: Evelyn Waugh, commenting on Henry Green's *Pack My Bag* (1940), remarked 'Only one thing disconcerted me . . . The proletarian grammar – the "likes" for "ases", the "bikes" for "bicycles", etc.'

'Both radio and television news agonizing over auxiliaries is a prevalent malaise.'

Alvar Lidell

A 16-year-old boy . . .
The campaign will be launched . . .
Trying to do the best *for* the country . . .
They are standing *by* their threat . . .

Such emphases should be avoided in formal broadcasts. In informal broadcasts they are not out of place if used in moderation. On the contrary, they have now become a major feature of modern spoken English, in unscripted contexts on the radio and TV, and in public speaking (e.g. in Parliament and the Law Courts), and represent a new feature of twentieth-century spoken English.

★ DEBATABLE FEATURES: PREFERENCES PROVIDED

1 *Use of 'who' and 'whom'*

(i) *Who* is the only relative pronoun that is declinable. In formal English *who* is normally the nominative and *whom* the oblique form, e.g.

It is you *who* are at fault.

Thanks to television, they know *who* I am.

The man *who* designed this building now lives in France.

A gardener of that name *whom* I once employed.

My grandfather *whom* I disliked and feared.

For *whom* the bell tolls.

I never met the person from *whom* I bought it.

(ii) An over-zealous search for correctness sometimes leads speakers to use *whom* in the wrong circumstances:

Take Sheikh Yamani *whom* (correctly *who*) they say is the richest man in the Middle East. (In this sentence the relative *who* is the subject of *is*, and *they say* is a parenthetical sentence inserted in the relative clause.)

Conversely, it is wrong to use the nominative *who* in such a case as:

They were a people *who* (correctly *whom*) it would be impossible to defeat.

(iii) In informal speech *who* sometimes quite naturally replaces *whom*. Thus a sentence like '*Who* do they think we are?', which is grammatically correct, leads to such unexceptionable sentences as '*Who* do you think you're talking to?' (*Very formal*: '*To whom* do you think you are talking?'). One well-known literary example showing an informal substitution of *who* for *whom* occurs in the works of Bernard Shaw: 'If it doesn't matter *who* anybody marries, then it doesn't matter *who* I marry and it doesn't matter *who* you marry.'

Preference: 'Who' and 'whom' should be carefully distinguished except in such informal circumstances as those indicated in (iii).

2 *Different from/to/than*

(i) The usual construction is now with *from* ('my policy is in no way different *from* yours'); but that with *to* (after *dissimilar to*) is found in writers of all periods:

> It's quite a different thing within *to* what it is without (Fielding).
>
> The party of prisoners lived . . . with comforts very different *to* those which were awarded to the poor wretches there (Thackeray).
>
> You'd find a rather different Moscow *to* Chekhov's (Graham Greene).

(ii) The construction with *than* (after *other than*) is found in Addison, Steele, Carlyle and Thackeray, among others, and is now common in American English:

> It is a different matter altogether *than* the one raised in the United Nations.

Preference: Use *different from* whenever possible; use *different to* only when it feels contextually natural (as when *dissimilar* or *similar* occurs nearby); avoid *different than*.

3 *Split infinitive*

(i) Infinitives have been split in English since at least the fourteenth century, and will continue to be split as time goes on, either for humorous effect (*Ross wants you to for God's sake stop attributing human behaviour to dogs* – James Thurber), or because of the awkwardness that can result from writing some sentences with unsevered infinitives.

Fowler divided English speakers into (1) those who neither know nor care what a split infinitive is; (2) those who do not know, but care very much; (3) those who know and condemn; (4) those who know and approve; and (5) those who know and distinguish.[1]

He went on to cite examples from Edwardian newspapers of high repute:

It will be found possible *to considerably improve* the present wages of the miners without jeopardizing the interests of capital.

Always providing that the Imperialists do not feel strong enough *to decisively assert* their power in the revolted provinces.

Because newspaper tradition is strongly against splitting it is perhaps fair to assume (he said) 'that each specimen is a manifesto of independence'.

(ii) Gradations of unnaturalness and ambiguity can be observed in the following:

Unnatural.	In not combining to forbid flatly hostilities.
Ambiguous.	In not combining flatly to forbid hostilities.
Unambiguous.	In not combining to flatly forbid hostilities.

Preference: Avoid splitting infinitives whenever possible but do not suffer undue remorse if a split infinitive is unavoidable for the natural and unambiguous completion of a sentence already begun.

A model example: *I wanted simply to tell you of my love* (Iris Murdoch).

4 *Misplacing of 'only'*

Only is often placed at a distance from the word or words it limits:

Where beasts were *only* slain for sacrifice (Dryden).

The eldest son shall *only* inherit his father's fortune (1721).

I *only* asked the question from habit (Jowett).

I *only* got wine by roaring for it (Evelyn Waugh).

I *only* met you at a party (Iris Murdoch).

---

1 *The Split Infinitive*, S.P.E. Tract No. xv, 1923.

In such contexts the stress and phrasing of the sentences normally prevent ambiguity in the spoken word but many listeners are adamant that such prosodic devices are inadequate.

Preference: Try to place *only* as near as possible to the word or words it limits. In scripted speech *only* should never be misplaced.

5 *Meaningless fillers*

These do not normally occur in scripted material but are not always avoidable in informal contexts and constitute useful rhythmical aids to speakers who temporarily lose their fluency:

actually	I mean to say
and er	really
and everything	sort of
and um	then ('Nice to talk to
didn't I ('I went	you, then')
into this shop,	um
didn't I?)	well now
er	you know
I mean	you see

Preference: It is obvious that too frequent a use of such fillers is undesirable, as in the following example:

'It's not really expensive. I mean, it only costs a pound.'

'It seems, sort of, a lot. I mean, when it used to cost only forty pence. I mean, where will it all end?'

'But, you know, forty pence then is like a pound now, and um, we must um make allowance for um inflation, and everything, if you know what I mean.'

6 *Other uses objected to by listeners*

Wrong sequence of tenses.

Strengthening of *I* by the addition of the word *myself*.

Use of *will/would* for *shall/should* as simple future tense.[1]

Confusion of *may* and *might*.[2]

None followed by a plural *verb*, e.g. *None of us are blameless.*

---

1 A convenient summary (but too long for inclusion here) of the main uses of these verbs can be found in *The Oxford Paperback Dictionary* s.v. *shall* and *should*.
2 Similarly s.v. *may* and *might*.

Preferences: In formal broadcasts such features can and should be avoided. In unscripted speech they will inevitably occur but should be kept to a minimum. The monitoring exercise revealed that such informal uses occurred far more frequently among interviewers than in the speech of BBC presenters and reporters.

INDEX OF SUBJECTS

INDEX OF WORDS